Crossings Over

THE CHESHIRE PRIZE FOR LITERATURE ANTHOLOGIES

Prize Flights: Stories from the Cheshire Prize for Literature 2003; edited by **Ashley Chantler**

Life Lines: Poems from the Cheshire Prize for Literature 2004; edited by **Ashley Chantler**

Word Weaving: Stories and Poems for Children from the Cheshire Prize for Literature 2005; edited by **Jaki Brien**

Edge Words: Stories from the Cheshire Prize for Literature 2006; edited by **Peter Blair**

Elements: Poems from the Cheshire Prize for Literature 2007; edited by **Peter Blair**

Wordscapes: Stories and Poems for Children from the Cheshire Prize for Literature 2008; edited by **Jaki Brien**

Zoo: Short Stories from the Cheshire Prize for Literature 2009; edited by **Emma Rees**

Still Life: Poetry from the Cheshire Prize for Literature 2010; edited by **Emma Rees**

Wordlife: Stories and Poems for Children from the Cheshire Prize for Literature 2011; edited by **Jaki Brien**

Lost and Found: Short Stories from the Cheshire Prize for Literature 2012; edited by **Emma Rees**

Great Escapes: Poetry from the Cheshire Prize for Literature 2013; edited by **Emma Rees**

Out of this Word: Stories and Poems for Children from the Cheshire Prize for Literature 2014; edited by **Jaki Brien**

Patches of Light: Short Stories from the Cheshire Prize for Literature 2015; edited by **Ian Seed**

Crossings Over

Poetry from the Cheshire Prize for Literature 2016

Edited by Ian Seed

University of Chester Press

First published 2017
by University of Chester Press
Parkgate Road
Chester CH1 4BJ

Printed and bound in the UK by the
LIS Print Unit
University of Chester
Cover designed by the LIS Graphics Team
University of Chester

Editorial Material
© University of Chester, 2017
Foreword and Poems
© the respective authors, 2017

All Rights Reserved
No part of this publication may be reproduced, stored in a retrieval system or transmitted in any form or by any means without the prior permission of the copyright owner, other than as permitted by UK copyright legislation or under the terms and conditions of a recognised copyright licensing scheme

A catalogue record of this book is available from the British Library

ISBN 978-1-908258-31-1

CONTENTS

Contributors	ix
Foreword	xxi
The Cartographer's Daughter *Cheryl Pearson*	1
The Water Dowser *Cheryl Pearson*	3
The Bone-Handled Knife *Jane Mack*	4
A June Afternoon *Brendan Flanagan*	6
Nantwich, Newcastle, Stratford-on-Avon *Nicki Griffin*	8
A Special Dispensation *Suzanne Iuppa*	10
Memories of a Good Plain Cook *Angi Holden*	12
Grandad's Arm *Gill McEvoy*	13

Crossings Over

The Change *Catherine Mark*	14
Bomb Crater 1943 *Sue Stern*	15
Dad: Latin at the Village School, 1969 *Helen Kay*	17
Portrait *Jan Dean*	19
Thomas Hardy by Lady Ottoline Morrell: Vintage Snapshot Print, Late 1924, National Portrait Gallery *Philip Howard*	21
Sloth *Sue Finch*	22
Jumping Endlessly for a Ball *Heather Freckleton*	23
Hawk Light *Peter Branson*	25
Sometime Before Myra Hindley *Angela Topping*	26

Contents

Palais de Danse 28
Richard Hughes

An Ending 29
Richard Hughes

Dusk Words 31
John Latham

Organ Lot 33
Andrew Rudd

Jodrell Bank Discovery Centre 35
Caroline Hawkridge

Visitors 37
Philip Williams

Legacy 39
Russell Morris

Tourist Trap 40
Duncan Brewer

Rubbish 42
Melanie Amri

Sweet Idleness 44
Frances Sackett

Crossings Over

Poets Cornered   45
Bruce Newman

Shakkei – Borrowed Scenery   47
Joy Winkler

Limited Edition   49
John Paul Davies

The Darkroom   51
John Paul Davies

CONTRIBUTORS

Melanie Amri gained a BA in Creative Writing with First Class Honours. Her work has appeared in literary magazines, including *Aesthetica* and *Mslexia*. In 2011, she won second prize in the *Mslexia* short story competition. In the same year, she was a winner in the *Real Story* competition. She has been longlisted for the International Rubery Short Story Award and the Fish Poetry Prize. In 2009 she was shortlisted by Screen West Midlands in their short film competition. An extract from her memoir, *Polar Regions, Desert Plains*, was published in the *Manchester Evening News*. Her work has been longlisted twice for BBC Radio 4 afternoon readings.

Peter Branson has lived in Cheshire for the last twenty-six years. A former teacher, lecturer and creative writing tutor, he is now a full-time poet, songwriter and traditional-style singer whose poetry has been published by journals in Britain, the USA, Canada, Ireland, Australasia and South Africa. He has won prizes and been placed in a number of poetry competitions in recent years, including a 'Highly Commended' in the Petra Kenny International, first prizes in the Grace Dieu and the *Envoi* International, a Special Commendation in the Wigtown, and the Silver Medal award in the 2016 Dermot Healy International Poetry Competition. *Red Hill: Selected*

Crossings Over

Poems 2000–2012 came out in 2013 with Lapwing (Belfast). His latest collection, *Hawk Rising*, was published in early April 2016 with the same publisher.

Duncan Brewer has worked as an investigative journalist and writer of science books for young people, and has been writing poetry with varying success for the last sixty years. He spends as much time as he can in Greece, which he finds to be a major source of poetic inspiration.

John Paul Davies is originally from Birkenhead, and now lives in County Meath, Ireland. His work has been published in *Orbis, Apex Magazine, The Fog Horn, Rosebud Magazine, The Pedestal Magazine, Pseudopod Poems,* and *Ares Magazine,* and is forthcoming from *Grain Magazine*. A poem of his is displayed in the finest pub in Liverpool, The Ship & Mitre.

Jan Dean is best known for her poetry for children. She has been shortlisted for the Centre for Literacy in Primary Poetry Award. *Reaching the Stars* – a celebration of the achievements of women – is a trio collaboration with Michaela Morgan and Liz Brownlee published with Macmillan in March 2017. She is a poet-in-schools and a National Poetry Day Ambassador for Forward Arts. Her poetry for adults has appeared in anthologies and magazines both online and in print.

Contributors

Sue Finch was born in Kent and grew up in Herne Bay. She has worked in primary education since 1993. She lives with her wife and enjoys exploring the countryside and coast as well as having days out at the zoo. Her first published poem appeared in *A New Manchester Alphabet* in 2015 whilst studying for her MA with Manchester Metropolitan University.

Brendan Flanagan, with roots in Northern Ireland and Liverpool, now lives in Rossendale, Lancashire. He has worked in Cheshire since 1993, based at Tatton Park and is now a senior manager with Cheshire East Council. His poetry, often inspired by his Irish roots, myths, landscapes, people and places, has been published in *The Reader* (No. 7, 2000), the Manchester Irish Writers' anthology *The Retting Dam* (2001), *Pennine Ink*, *Passing Clouds* and on the internet.

Heather Freckleton has lived in numerous locations in the UK and spent a short time in India. She now lives in Hull, the 2017 UK City of Culture. She has won many prizes for her poetry and short stories and has appeared in various anthologies. She feels compelled to write even though this can feel like wading through mud wearing a heavy backpack! She is looking forward to more dreaming and writing and just fitting all the other stuff in.

Nicki Griffin is from Nantwich, Cheshire, and now lives in County Clare, Ireland. Her poetry has been published in a variety of journals and anthologies. Her debut collection of poetry, *Unbelonging*, was published by Salmon Poetry in 2013 and was shortlisted for the Shine/Strong Poetry Award 2014 for best debut collection. *The Skipper & Her Mate* (non-fiction) was published by New Island in 2013. Her second collection of poetry is due in 2017. She is co-editor of the poetry newspaper *Skylight 47*.

Caroline Hawkridge manages innovative literary projects via The Hawkridge Agency. These include Simon Armitage's two walks as a modern troubadour, her work for *Deaths of the Poets* by Paul Farley and Michael Symmons Roberts (2017) and the fun of being 'fungi' poet-in-residence for the National Aspergillosis Centre. Caroline's own books include *Understanding Endometriosis*, the first British book for women on this health problem. It sold worldwide for eighteen years. Recently, Caroline won *Mslexia's* Villanelle Challenge. *The Dark Horse* nominated her for the Forward Prize for Best Single Poem. Her poems have been runner-up in the Cheshire Prize for Literature (Children), Highly Commended by the *Magma*, York and Torbay competitions, published in a variety of magazines and anthologised by Candlestick Press.

Angi Holden is a Lecturer in Creative Writing and freelance writer, whose work includes prizewinning adult and children's poetry, short stories and flash

Contributors

fictions, published in online and print anthologies. She brings a wide range of personal experience to her writing, alongside a passion for lifelong learning. Her family is central to her life, and her research into family history is a significant influence on her work. She was the winner of the inaugural Mother's Milk Books Pamphlet Prize and her pamphlet, *Spools of Thread* will be published by Mother's Milk Books in 2017.

Philip Howard works for Preston City Council. As a practising poet, he would like to see poetry restored as an art form which can be appreciated by all through relevant and accessible work that tackles compelling subject matter. Some of his newer poetry has been published in various anthologies such as *The Stony Thursday Book* and *Inspired by my Museum* (the latter of which was a poem inspired by the Harris Museum's iconic portrait, 'Pauline in the Yellow Dress'). His poems have also featured on websites such as *The Health of the North* and *The Film Mag,* on a Park Trail in Yorkshire and in poetry magazines such as *Snakeskin, Decanto* and *Prole.*

Originally from Seven Sisters in Glamorgan, **Richard Hughes** has worked in education, broadcasting and as librarian and proofreader for Ilford Ltd. For two years he struggled to sell second-hand books. In recent years his poems have been published in *Acumen, The Interpreter's House, Other Poetry, Orbis,*

SOUTH and *The Frogmore Papers*. In the Erbacce Poetry Prize 2014 he achieved joint third place. He was shortlisted for the Frogmore Poetry Prize 2014, gained third place in the Mere Literary Prize 2014 and managed joint first for the Orbis 165 Readers' Award.

Suzanne Iuppa is a poet, community worker and conservationist who lives in Snowdonia National Park, North Wales. She was raised on Lake Ontario and moved to the UK in the 1980s, studying Modern British Poetry and Countryside Management. Her work can be found in many British and American literary magazines and anthologies, and she has two published series: *On Track: Poems from Welsh Pilgrimage* (Alyn Books, 2013) and *Wellspring* (The Gwendraeth Press, 2015). She spent many years working as a forestry officer in Cheshire and was the Chair of Chester Writers in 2014–2016. Suzanne also makes short films, and secret gardens.

Helen Kay has had poems published in various magazines and her debut pamphlet, *The Poultry Lover's Guide to Poetry*, was published last year by Indigo Dreams. She has five hens and works as a part-time dyslexia tutor.

John Latham was Professor of Physics at the University of Manchester for several decades and is now Senior Visiting Scientist at the National Center for Atmospheric Research in Boulder, Colorado, USA.

Contributors

With a team of about twenty-five scientists and engineers he is studying a novel idea for combating global warming that he first published in 1990 in the journal *Nature*. He has published six books of poetry, one novel, and has won first prize in about twenty-five UK poetry competitions.

Jane Mack is a Chester Guide and shows visitors around the city on walking tours in English and French. She has retired from tutoring at West Cheshire College, where she taught French and Italian to adults. After gaining an MPhil on 'A Critical Study of the Poetry and Prose of Laurie Lee' from the University of Manchester (1995), she wrote the Introduction to *Laurie Lee: Three Plays* (2003) as a result of further research. Jane has written poetry for many years and won a runner-up prize in the National Poetry Competition in 1988. She is a member of various writing and reading groups, and hopes to have a collection of poems published later this year.

Catherine Mark, of Nigerian heritage, grew up in the Middle East and studied in the West. After working as a teacher of English Language and Literature for almost a decade, she is now a curate at All Saints Parish Church, Streetly, in the West Midlands. In 2010, she was awarded an MA in Creative Writing with distinction from Manchester Metropolitan University and is currently completing a PhD. She writes poetry and short stories, and is working on her first novel as part of her doctoral studies. Her microfictions, 'The Killing' and 'Uncle Blessing', were published by Commonword in the anthology, *Elevator Fiction* in 2016.

Gill McEvoy has published two full collections with Cinnamon Press, and three pamphlets with Happenstance Press, the most recent of which, *The First Telling*, won the Michael Marks Award in 2015. In 2016 she was poet-in-residence at Harvard's Centre for Hellenic Studies, Nafplio, Greece. Gill is a Hawthornden Fellow.

Russell Morris is a fine artist, painter, printmaker and poet. His poetry has been published by Commonword Press of Manchester and also in previous anthologies for the Cheshire Prize for Literature. His current exhibition project combines poetry, drawings and monoprints. Entitled 'All The Days She Can Spare', it charts his mother's decline through Alzheimer's, and includes this year's competition entry, 'Legacy'. It has toured from Clun in South Shropshire to Chester Cathedral, then Keele University, and is to be included as part of the Spring–Summer programme at the Bleddfa Centre in Radnorshire in mid-Wales.

Bruce Newman had a career in market research, sales and marketing before retiring in September 2012. He then became interested in writing and is an active

Contributors

member of Castle Park Writers in Frodsham. He also took up art and tennis, but admits that recognition for his watercolours and his sporting prowess could take a long time! As a West Ham supporter he has learned to take nothing for granted. He is married to Lorraine, has three sons and lives in Helsby.

Cheryl Pearson lives and writes in South Manchester. Her poems have appeared in publications including *The Guardian, Neon, Crannóg, Envoi, Antiphon*, and *The Compass Magazine*. She won third prize in the Bare Fiction Poetry Competition 2016, and has been shortlisted for the York Literature Festival Poetry Competition and the Princemere Poetry Prize. She has also been nominated for a Pushcart Prize. Her first full collection *Oysterlight* was published in March 2017 with Pindrop Press.

Andrew Rudd lives in Frodsham, Cheshire, and was Cheshire Poet Laureate in 2006. His poetry collections are *One Cloud Away from the Sky* (2007) and *Nowhere Else but Here* (2012). He was the winner of the Cheshire Prize for Literature in 2004 and 2007. He was selected as one of the Aldeburgh Eight – for an intensive writing week in Suffolk – in 2015. He is constantly amazed by the intricacy and beauty of the smallest and most ordinary things, and sometimes writes about them.

Frances Sackett's poetry has been published widely in magazines and journals in the UK and Canada. She was a tutor in Poetry for the University of Manchester's Courses for the Public for six years, a founder member of Marple Writers, and part of a project in 2016 to write poems about Manchester Cathedral. Her poems also appear in *Welsh Women's Poetry 1460–2001* (Honno Welsh Women's Classics) and *Parents* (Enitharmon Editions). Her book, *The Hand Glass* is published by Seren.

Sue Stern writes poetry and fiction for children and adults. She has an MA in Children's Fiction/Novel Writing from Manchester Metropolitan University. Her poetry and short stories have appeared in journals and anthologies in Britain and America. Red Bank Books published her middle-grade novel, *Rafi Brown and the Candy Floss Kid*, in 2013. She has recently completed *My Blue-Eyed Girl*, a memoir of Vanessa, her beautiful charismatic daughter, who though profoundly disabled by cerebral palsy, transformed Sue's life. Set in Manchester and Cheshire during the 1960s and 70s, the book also chronicles more positive attitudes towards disability and significant improvements in women's lives in the areas of maternity and childbirth. Sue is now seeking publication of the memoir.

Angela Topping's eighth full collection, *The Five Petals of Elderflower*, was published in 2016 by Red

Contributors

Squirrel Press. She is also the author of five chapbooks and several critical works, the most recent of which, on the poet John Clare, came out in 2015 from Greenwich Exchange. Poems have appeared in *Poetry Review*, *The Dark Horse* and many other magazines, and in over seventy anthologies. In 2013, she was a writer-in-residence at Gladstone's Library. A former teacher, she has contributed chapters to several Creative Writing textbooks, and co-authored three GCSE textbooks. She now works freelance as a poet.

Joy Winkler is a former Cheshire Poet Laureate who works freelance as a writer, poet and workshop leader. Following the success of her verse-drama *TOWN*, her new play, *Lightning under their Skirts*, with director Kevin Dyer, toured the North West in May 2017. It is a Storm in the North production with Action Transport Theatre, supported by The National Lottery through Arts Council England. Joy is also the author of four poetry collections, most recently *Stolen Rowan Berries*, and has been published in several anthologies. Joy has facilitated creative writing in many community settings, including HMP Styal, Salford's Writing Lives and for Cartwheel Arts. Currently, she is running public workshops at the National Trust's Tatton Park.

Philip Williams grew up in South Wales, was briefly a 'Ten Pound Pom' in 1960s Australia and spent many years in Yorkshire. He has lived in Alsager for ten years and is married with two student daughters. He won the High Sheriff's Cheshire Prize in 2013 and his poetry has appeared in *Agenda*, *Iota*, *Planet* and regional anthologies. He runs a regular Poems & Pints session in Alsager and is a member of the Poetry Society's Stoke Stanza. He works freelance in marketing and marketing research and has his finger in all sorts of unpaid pies. He likes the pastry.

Ian Seed (Editor) is Lecturer in Creative Writing, and Programme Leader for the BA in Creative Writing, at the University of Chester. His poetry, short stories, articles and translations have appeared in numerous journals and anthologies, including *The Forward Book of Poetry 2017* (Faber & Faber) and *The Best British Poetry 2014* (Salt). He is the author of a number of collections of poetry. His latest book, *Identity Papers*, was published by Shearsman in February 2016 and was featured on BBC Radio 3's *The Verb*.

FOREWORD

The poems gathered in this anthology make me think of small, yet hardy vessels navigating their way across choppy, hazardous waters. They take us with them over to the other side, and when we look back we can hardly believe the voyage we have made. Yet somehow they have kept us safe and brought us to a fresh understanding of our lives.

There are many different kinds of poem here, crossing back and forth, making a rich tapestry of voices, opening new ways into those areas which have always been the territory of poetry: love, death, nature, relationships, age, politics, and indeed poetry itself. They encompass a wide range of tone, from regretful to celebratory, lyrical to comic, dramatic to reflective. Each of the poems tells a story, or rather *shows* us a story, since poetry so often thinks in imagery. The poems also cross over to one another in a kind of ongoing dialogue. When putting this anthology together, I was astonished by the different connections and relationships that emerge between them. Every poem here stands on its own, yet as we read on (best done out loud), the different voices combine to make a choral one.

Shelley famously said that poets are the 'unacknowledged legislators of the world'. The twentieth-century poet George Oppen added that 'poets are the legislators of the unacknowledged world'. This is especially true of contemporary poetry and of many of the poems in *Crossings Over*. They are not afraid to investigate those matters we can find so difficult to talk about in our everyday lives. And yet they are never rarefied or otherworldly. They open us up to what we already know but all too readily fail to recognise.

One of the qualities that I admire about these poems is the way that they work at different levels. This is especially true of the overall winner, 'The Cartographer's Daughter' by Cheryl Pearson. With its imagery and narrative, 'The Cartographer's Daughter' has all the feel of an epic novel. When we have finished reading the poem (again, best out loud), it may well seem to us that we have made an immense journey, and yet the journey has been made in just twenty-four lines. At the same time, 'The Cartographer's Daughter' is a deeply personal and moving lyrical poem. In terms of form, it is a poem which takes risks with its sprawling lines and daring line breaks. This is all part of the dangerous crossing over. In the hands of a lesser poet, we would have floundered and sunk long before we reached the other side.

'The Cartographer's Daughter' was selected for first prize from a very high number of entries. It was agreed upon unanimously by the judges. Choosing the three runners-up was no easy challenge. It took a long discussion over endless coffees in the University of Chester's Senate House to come to an agreement. The standard of many of the entries was exceptionally high,

Foreword

and came in a rich variety of theme, style and form. Eventually, however, we came to our decision. The three runners-up (in alphabetical order by surname) are: John Paul Davies with 'Darkroom', Helen Kay with 'Dad: Latin at the Village School, 1969' and Joy Winkler with 'Shakkei – Borrowed Scenery'.

I would like to offer my thanks to my fellow judges: John Scrivener, long-standing judge of the Cheshire Prize for Literature, and Dr William Stephenson, prizewinning poet in his own right. Their invaluable help in the judging process and in making the final selections for the prizes, as well as in making suggestions for the anthology, has made all the difference. This anthology would not be here without them. I am grateful to the High Sheriff of Cheshire, Kathy Cowell OBE, for announcing the winners' names, presenting them with their prizes, and helping to make the awards evening such an enjoyable and informative one.

My thanks to the distinguished poet and radio broadcaster, Ian McMillan, for reading out the winning entry at the awards evening, for sharing his own work with the audience, and for speaking so engagingly about the different elements that come into play when making a poem.

I appreciate more than a little all the assistance I have had from the University of Chester's Corporate Communications team, especially the patience and advice of Jayne Dodgson and Jenni Westcott, while Sarah Griffiths, as managing editor for the University of Chester Press, has been exceptionally helpful at each step of the way. I would also like to thank Emma Shipman from Learning and Information Services for capturing much of the spirit of *Crossings Over* with the cover design and the Print Unit for producing the anthologies.

Finally, my thanks to the poets themselves. It has been a privilege to collect your poems in this anthology.

Ian Seed
Chair Judging Panel, and Editor, *Crossings Over*,
Department of English, University of Chester,
May 2017

THE CARTOGRAPHER'S DAUGHTER

Cheryl Pearson

He brought the world to the kitchen table –
unceremonious, a small square he lifted out of itself,
two wings beating away from that centre crease.
Again, it opened, and again, like a wild goose
breaking out of winter, chasing light. Until all seven
    continents replaced
the knuckled oak, my mother's plates,
an ocean in the place of water glasses, cups.
How we travelled, fingertip by fingertip. I rubbed the
    deserts thin
with my camel hands. He obliterated France with his
    thumbs. Once,
he drew two dragons over Spain at my request, red
    and rearing,
barking flames. I learned history from his knee, I
    learned geography.
I learned that there are maps which are not paper
    maps,
but exist in the body, its seas of blood, and lines of
    memory.
The word childhood, and I am back: those golden
    afternoons
with my father, a pan of milk rolling to a boil, and the
    fine net

of latitudes and longitudes, the flat blue box of oceans
    and bitten coasts.
When he died, I knew to map my grief, that naming it
    would keep me
found. I brought out the old square, brown
and thin as onionskin, and let its dry wings open. *An
    adoration
of mountains*, I thought. *An inheritance of seas.*
I held my new daughter, blood of my blood, blood of
    his.
Hushed her curdling cries until she calmed. There,
when she stilled, and smiled: the lines of his face,
a map going all the way back to the stars.

THE WATER DOWSER

Cheryl Pearson

Running through generations like a river, alongside
the gene for red hair, and the family name: this gift
of summoning the earth's weather. A humming
in the wrists, is how he describes it. I picture his
    hands,
like knuckles of ginger, thrumming with bees: tiny
    harbingers
browsing his tributaries, raising the alarm
in the hand/arm hinge. In the old days, they called it
witching the water; walked their switch of hazel,
    switch of willow,
waited for the dip and twitch that meant they'd
    struck gold
and clear-running cold would follow. Years ago, I
    saw a palmist
on a seaside pier. Watched her winnow a future from
    the forks
of my hands. Believed in magic. Now, I stand in a
    dry field watching
a man draw water like doves from his sleeves. *Some
    people
don't believe in this*, he tells me, spits, then grins. I
    think of moons,
salt lines in the sand. Of my blood, going out,
    coming in.

THE BONE-HANDLED KNIFE

Jane Mack

As I hold
the bone-handled knife
and slowly spread

these rough-hewn
slices of bread, I am there
in that Kentish kitchen,

looking up
through the window to a crescendo
of cowslips beyond

the 'elephant grave',
that wide, rotund rockery
separating them

from the lawn below
where a song-thrush tugs
at a worm.

As I hold
the bone-handled knife
I feel the pulse

of your hand,
your flesh around the bone
and you

are here, here
in my kitchen, slowly spreading
the bread.

A JUNE AFTERNOON

Brendan Flanagan

The afternoon wore on.
My father picked stones
That cropped like potatoes
Among the weak tremblings
Of an infant lawn,
Washing pegged on the line
Untroubled by the faint
Chance of a sun-shower.

I sat by a slow stream
With a punctured crust
On its dry mud bank
In a field off the Burren road.

He lay finger-caged,
Red-throated pouted kiss
Blown in an alien mist,
Flicker-light slowly fading
As cage became cup and
Cup became a beggar's hands,
A draining, sorrowful mount
Reverently framed.

Sail-struck stickleback,
Beached schooner
De-masted and alone
Scared as a fish can be.

I showed little purpose
In this unholy baptism
Other than the power
Which bathes in the glory
Of self-righteous control,
That keeps spiders in matchboxes
And harvests frog-spawn
From the very same stream.

He tried to speak
But I could not hear him.
As I tilted my hands
He slipped silently away.

NANTWICH, NEWCASTLE, STRATFORD-ON-AVON
(after Kim Moore)

Nicki Griffin

I come from people who stitched garments for a
    living,
who rented terraced houses on narrow streets
or shared rooms in four-storey houses.
People who believed women who drank
in pubs had loose morals, who raised their children
to believe in God, Church of England variety,
sent them unrelentingly to Sunday School.
My Uncle Fred built the black-and-white telly,
watched the racing, liked a flutter. Auntie Ev
had a calliper and a tongue sharp as a paper cut.

I come from people who kept a maid to do the work
they didn't want to, whose house belonged to them
not a landlord, who went to Chapel, worshipped
a Methodist God. They didn't mind women
being theatrical or taking a nap in the afternoon.
Farmers, coal merchants, builders of ships.
Some of their stories muddied the trail of ancestors
they'd rather not have. Auntie Bea went to America,
Jenny disappeared Down Under.

When my two people came together, one side
didn't think well of the other.
Friends told him he should marry someone else.
He told them where to go.
She worked on her telephone voice,
stopped calling people love,
warned me not to play with the common girls
up the road. Mine were people who didn't bring
    things
into the open, kept the wounds stitched tight.

A SPECIAL DISPENSATION

Suzanne Iuppa

A special dispensation

for my aunts in their knee-socks, caught with buck
 teeth
used to eating only fish on Fridays.

For the large bottle of Maalox the guide kept topside
equally scanning Grandma's skirt and the Seaway

everyone praying for the bacon not to come back in
 waves.
For the islands, at once Canadian, and American,

cold for August. Pine-tattooed and saturated –
my grandfather's Kodachrome slides outliving

many of us; digitised, then shared,
the remainder instantly falling for face recognition.
 Scrolling

furrows of vacationers and fashion shades and tinted
 glass …

For our immigrant status, not comprehending duty-
    free
nor the ambush strategy of the northern pike.

For my family, not too fazed by yesterday's hooks.

MEMORIES OF A GOOD PLAIN COOK

Angi Holden

'There's a bottle in the pantry, near the back' she'd
    said,
her slender fingers spread across the open page

of Delia, or Marguerite, or Graham Kerr. And so
    there was.
We found it when we cleared the shelves: hot
    Mexican Tabasco

lodged like a single thought amongst the jumbled
    gelatine
and Maraschino cherries, the olives stuffed with
    garlic cloves,

the Lea & Perrins past its sell-by date
(who would have guessed it might go off?)

sea salt, cane sugar, angelica and pots of herbs that
    once
held promises of fennel, bay and tarragon. Strange
    then

that we remember Shepherd's Pie and Golden Syrup
    Sponge,
the nursery food she now consumes, spoon fed.

GRANDAD'S ARM

Gill McEvoy

When he explained about the arm
that hung so useless by his side
I only heard the word he used
and thought immediately
of how it was the sound of pebbles
shovelled up the beach –
shrap, shrap, shrap –
the slap of waves as they collapsed
then the lulling sound
as they withdrew –
nelnelnel.

I am ashamed to think now
of those metal splinters in his flesh,
the way he winced each time
I tried to hug him tight.

THE CHANGE

Catherine Mark

Ball of string lodged in throat.
Took nine months
to breathe,
to cough,
not choke –
dislodge the knotted mass

cull nine weeks of being with child.
Amelia. Noah. Freya.
Expanded breast sacs,
bloated abdominal tissue –
Sudden. Gone. Numb.

Hand rubs emptied cave,
remembers bloodied mess.
Pug-faced counsellor
tugs at the string of silent
emotions locked in –

loosens
pulls
until
the words form and fall
in waves of grief.

BOMB CRATER 1943

Susan Stern

I'm walking through the field
making sure the snails don't get me
singing to myself about the sunshine.
Bryan Jeffcote who lives next door, walks in front,
David Jeffcote who lives next door, walks behind
    him.
I'm the last. They've got white hair
because their Mummy gives them marge
and eats the butter ration. Everyone knows that.
They bang the path with sticks
until we reach the bomb crater
then run down banging the ground
and the little stones run after them.

I slide down the side
and the little stones slide with me.
Now the walls are up to the sky.
I can't see the hen house. I can't see Mummy
hanging out the washing.
Bryan and David hit the bluebells
with their sticks. Bryan says David is a German.
David says he isn't. They have a sword fight.
Bryan stands in front of me. David stands in front of
    me.

They're high as the walls of the bomb crater.
They say show me your bum. So I do.

Stones fall on my head on my arms
on my legs. Someone is running
someone picks me up and carries me to the top.
It's Daddy. My face is pressed
so hard into his jacket I can't see.
Something is banging in his chest like the banging
yesterday, when I was sitting on his knee
and he shouted at Mummy.
And she cried.

Daddy, you're walking too quickly,
Daddy, I want to get down.

DAD: LATIN AT THE VILLAGE SCHOOL, 1969

Helen Kay

Amo. No John and Janet picnics here,
No hoops or fish or tambourines. A chain
Of mopheads decks the furrowed desks.
It hides a mottled row of knuckle knees.
Amas. The head dictates a verb, looks through
The window. Naked oaks scratch phlegmy clouds.

Amat. Tom's pen is harrowing the lines.
In sneaks the demon, dislocates his arm.
The nib injects the paper. Ink puddles
While Titivillus skins each page of words
Then tips the pelts inside his sniggering sack,
And opens out umbrella wings to leave.

Now Tom's a statue on his chair again.
Tears blot his face and urine scribes his calves.
He must decline a new verb, *smarto, smartet.*
His brothers ache to help, fester, afraid,
In scabs of silence. Their dad works on the farms.
His fists can't dent a teacher's slick defence.

The school won prizes for calligraphy.
His MBE could not absolve the head.
He was struck off; the tabloids loved the story.
It's rumoured spirits smashed his gravestone.
Tom is mute, boxed in his barking tractor.
A hairy hand has wiped away his version.

PORTRAIT

Jan Dean

I am on Uncle Harry's table
but he is not my uncle
and it is not a table
it is a studio block

someone has lifted me up and sat me down
arranged me with a doll kitted out in green
knitted cardie   pixie bonnet
tied under the chin with thin wool string

my cotton dress is smocked
my ankle socks are neatly cuffed
my hair in fat and separate curls
as if a flock of bubbles has settled on my head

everything around me is pale grey twill
and I am more still
than all the pyramids of tins
in our shop window

I must stay still for a million minutes
wriggling is forbidden
I may not move the doll

the shutter clicks
again-again   again-again
a sound like metal shortbread snapping
and then we're done

I lift the doll
pull off her head
to see what makes her eyelids close

my father mends her later
but she's not the same
her glance skew-whiff for ever more

THOMAS HARDY
BY LADY OTTOLINE MORRELL:
VINTAGE SNAPSHOT PRINT, LATE 1924,
NATIONAL PORTRAIT GALLERY

Philip Howard

Perhaps it was just a case of happenstance
That a rich celebrity aristo
Had her camera handy, purely chance?

I doubt that we shall ever really know
His take on it as he struck that stiff pose,
Gladioli in the vase at his elbow;

It's not a case of looking down his nose
At us, it's more an ironic look, wry,
More like poetry than straightforward prose.

Who knows? Perhaps he was asking himself, why:
Why the hoo-ha over 'Jude the Obscene',
The vitriol and the public outcry,

The venting of censorious rage and spleen?
Or were they fatalistic thoughts of life,
Of the untold story that might have been
Had she lived, Emma, his grieved-for first wife?

SLOTH

Sue Finch

Looking up she points you out.
Untidy ball
suspended by overlong claws
that I swear are made from mahogany.
Hooked we stare.
We think we see you move
but it is the dizziness in our blood
from craning necks, refocusing eyes,
that twitches, not you.
We are willing you to flex;
you, our shooting star in hypnotic sky,
we do not dare to blink.
Yet your face stays
nestled in bed-headed fur.
Your hot breath clouds around your nose
moistening the dusty twigs caught in your coat
with the hay-like scent of eaten leaves.
You are brewing
an intoxicating sleeping potion.
We too will slow
if we stay and watch.
A damp green smell rises from the terrapin pool.
Remembering algae can grow on you
I turn to leave.

JUMPING ENDLESSLY FOR A BALL

Heather Freckleton

Dog; odd eared, string tailed, provenance unknown
is never asked, Who the hell are you?
Which might be about borders and bombs,
     passports,
papers, binds of any kind and could bring to mind,
Who the hell am I? When your photos are always
of the past and the world's mirror
has blurred your edges.

I watch the dog jump endlessly for a ball
body curved in air, the thwack of ball in mouth.
She brings, she drops, I throw
we have a rhythm going.

Dog has an odour of grease and other creatures
out of reach like the wolf not bad
but misunderstood who might bring wildness
to my door, break into my dream, show me things
I almost understand while night, low-bellied
loiters in the yard.

Dog dives beneath brambles, takes messages
from grasses, treads mosses, rocks, and sinks in sand.
I remember these things when the world rings
with news as dark as burning
earth and the image of a child face down
in water won't go away. In my mind
I endlessly throw a ball, watch
dog's graceful jump, her turning in the air
all her beginnings and endings there.

How should a life be lived?

I watch the dog streaking the land
as if it had no end
stopping in moments, nose up
breathing everything in.
I stand, ready, ball in hand.

HAWK LIGHT

('Hawk-light' – when there is enough morning light
for the hawk to begin to hunt)

Peter Branson

Three quarter's day, watch jackdaws drift
crow-high like ashes from a pyre.
Light rationing, what is dissolved
in mistle-morning air to might-
have-beens beyond the kissing gate,
the magpie's rattled afterthought
resolves pipe dream to motherlode,
the slipstream of a silver ghost.
Sheer featherweight, a sickle blade
scything turf-high, last second writhe,
shape-shifting, curves space-time to shave
the hedge-top, element surprise,
pure guile, to mantle living flesh
and thrive, fierce yellow eyes on fire.

SOMETIME BEFORE MYRA HINDLEY

Angela Topping

Even now I wonder, was I right about him,
the man who asked us if we'd like to see his rabbits?
I'd heard whispers of kids being *interfered with*.

The older girl, minding me, wanted to go with him
but I knew wild rabbits wouldn't wait for us
and who takes a hutch on to waste-ground at night?

I was wrapped in a scarf of mother's fears,
with spells knitted tight against the dark,
and pinned to my vest was the holy scapular.

'Don't go with him! Run for the fair!'
Although *my mother said I never should
go with the gypsies*, it was only a rhyme.

We ran across the road to brassy lights:
the Wurlitzer, bobbing ducks, pink candy floss,
past the gun range, looking for a stranger to trust.

Men had urges, couldn't help themselves.
We'd been told a woman could never hurt us,
though we should never get into anyone's car.

The dodgem woman hurried us to St Marie's,
rang the priest's bell, gabbled our story.
Our mothers cried when they came to collect us.

Walking home past waste-ground newly fenced
where he'd said his rabbits lived, I'd see,
    unreachable
through wire mesh, an orange plastic ball.

PALAIS DE DANSE

Richard Hughes

He thinks he storms the people's palace.
Smoother than velvet his Brylcreem charm
brings a flush to plush décor, his blue eyed
steady gaze makes the soft lights wobble.
The maple floor concedes to his touch.
The band stands up and takes notice.

In truth, each week beneath the glitterball
they line up to turn him down. He hates
their hand-stitched skirts, their pert breasts
held by bras dipped in sugar water; he hates
the slow swirl of the all-seeing globe,
a mosaic of their winking eyes.

AN ENDING

Richard Hughes

The special yoke-shaped pillow
brings no comfort. She shifts
in her chair, pushes, pulls
its corners. No good. We whisper advice
but she's not listening.

Travel-lagged, I'm impatient
for the cosy wrap of home routine.

We help her to dress. It takes an age
to slip each arm into its cardigan sleeve.
Her eyes flick to ceiling corners
where loops of spent cobwebs dangle.

Later my aunts insist we take turns
at the bedside but I get the call
before my shift is due. The end comes
with a slight flinch, a frown, an intake
of breath like a reversed sigh.

As we sit on, the ruby tassels
and low wash of the bedside lamp
bring to mind my old nights of sickness

when, feverish and restless,
I lay hugging the certainty
that beyond the night-light,
the half-open bedroom door,
the landing and quiet stairs,
the lit door frame
she was there;
her voice a shawl, a lullaby, a castle wall.

DUSK WORDS

John Latham

In my sleepless bed I find a perfect word
mirroring exactly the language of the night
its mutterings, nuances, random traffic,

but it fades away and is lost to me by dawn.
No matter, sufficient that this word exists
and might return someday to reinforce

black's whisperings, its populated silence:
while I, retreating from the daylight world
snuggle into dark, the Earth's deep breathing.

Sometimes I find words that rhyme with ones
I'm searching for: *rapacious* not *capacious*,
contusion not *confusion*, *spurn* instead of *yearn*.

If I struggle to retrieve them, they don't return,
for Heisenberg was right – we alter everything
we see or touch. On my last lap now, forgetting

whom I've dialed or, when they answer, who
I am: leaving the gas-flame on: or driving home
to a house I moved out of, forty years ago.

My history remains in me, but I can't grasp
or share it. Fragments visit me in dreams, these
my real life now. Outside of them I am not me.

Words' sounds more powerful than meanings.
Sorrel, not a colour but shade at lemon times,
Sorrel, the dog or cat I shared with whom?

Those I most want at this 90-candle party
all dead. But you still here, forgotten friends
who won't stop trying: Oh yes, you will do.

I'm not afraid of it, not much, not yet,
but I can feel it coming, the dawning dark,
wisps of altostratus that subdue the sun

and in their fleeting passage shiver me.
Ripple-widow, herbal craft, scrape hollow.
My clock lingers at eleven. Midnight soon.

ORGAN LOT

Andrew Rudd

The road turns, sweeps downhill
past this two-acre field, the Organ Lot,
whose rent was used to pay the organist.

I imagine a thread – it spools out
from this patch of ground, between trees,
past settlements of the living,

across the churchyard, in through the huge
oak door, to the organ stool. So that,
sustained by this soft ripple of barley,

these few cattle clustered with their calves,
these cartloads of corn, the chancel might
resound with *Magnificat* (Set B, after Handel)

though in a lean year, there'd be scarcely
enough to fund a Lenten dirge.

*

The Quinquennial report's arrived. More lead
ripped from the roof, rain pouring in.

Two youths have broken through the vestry
door, taking turns to star in the CCTV

as they take up the offering. The trustees
meet with another glass or two

of Tony Jolly's ale, steady themselves
for the latest bill. How to restore

the damaged pipes and levers?
How to eke out this field

for another harvest? I want so much
to believe this line will hold.

This unpretentious grass, the thankful
people as they come.

JODRELL BANK DISCOVERY CENTRE

Caroline Hawkridge

You are a kestrel in October, sky bubbled
through your bones, eye knotted to the verge.

Every vole has Ariadne's gift: how to mark
the way home in the tussocky labyrinth.

You can detect their trails: ultraviolet-dark urine
drip-painted beside the road.

Here you will whisk on the retinas of drivers,
this evening's audience. They may notice

something or nothing,
as the wind tries to raise a tune

along the comb and paper of your wings.
Now and then, your black cuff tail will tilt.

Our compere says that the radio telescope could
    hunt
a mobile phone left on silent on Mars.

I watch you speck our view of the dish,
its paraboloid, cobweb. Phones are shut down.

A poet rises to the stage beside *Our Place in the
    Universe.*
We are all ears – cartilage cups, tympanums,

ossicles – struck by waves of his sound.
The dish goes on listening to silence.

VISITORS

Philip Williams

I met the Satyr in my garden, sat
on the stone-bench beside the pond,
gave him my spare pair of shorts
for when we went to town.

I bought him a skinny latte,
a bowl of olives, asked him
how he'd arrived here undetected:
all muscle on the bench presses
and bar-bells at the gym,
hair and horn and woolly thighs,
hoof beats on the pavements trotting.

He drew out his double-flute, grinned,
began to play a reedy drone,
soon set us all to dancing –
the woman with pushchair and toddler,
the man cornered with dreams, debt and laptop,
surly teenagers, Facebook silver-surfers
all dancing.

Trip-trap, trip-trap.
We clicked our fingers, felt the tap
on the off-beat chiming, the precinct's reel
and pull as we wound outside – thank goodness
for his shorts – where we stepped and jogged,
foot to foot, heel to toe, sleek handbags slung
on chair-backs, dancing.

The Centaur joined us from the Turf Accountants,
all rippling flanks, a mean tambourine.
Drivers left their cars, cyclists propped
their bikes on railings, peeled off lycra.
We skipped and sang through selfie flares,
Ocado horns, police sirens wailing.

LEGACY

Russell Morris

Choosing to leave this and not that behind
from the massed inconsequential:
biscuit tins of postcards unwritten,
the picture-books of stately homes,
thirty yards of fine green baize still upon the roll.

Beyond the edge of town there are holes in which to
    pour the pity of these things:
your life-slide, your torrent;
where at some point it must all be as rags, broken
    china and dust.

But against this great reduction,
the breaking, tearing and discarding
which the stuff of your past will be subjected to
I will promise not to be careless with your memory.

So I will make a room as the Egyptians once did,
where things might be folded, hung, or set neatly in
    cupboards
with dried lavender
cut from the bushes that once lined the path to your
    door.

TOURIST TRAP

Duncan Brewer

The wild citizens cursing the tank crews
were their own fathers and mothers.
A clean morning, tasty air, no traffic.
Sailors in a jeep collared me
walking to the harbour,
could tell me nothing,
finally gave me bread and sardines,
sent me to hole up
in a waterfront doss house
with beggars and street musicians,
who sat on the roof listening
to the crackle and pop
of gunfire in the curfew dark.

And with the light I caught
the last ferry to the islands,
where I stewed for months in sun and sea
and my landlord praised the soldiers
for suppressing anarchy, and the postman
basked in his role as censor,
and fishermen and farmers muttered
but got on with it, because they know
the world is run by colonels and ship owners,
and one day I found teeth and skull fragments
breaking the surface near an ancient cemetery,

but the grave goods were long gone, and
labouring back along the sand, I met
a deaf and dumb man leading
a bull calf, who gave me
half a cucumber to quench my thirst –
and my memories of most days are of
heat, and salt and acid fruit, and
the night-time scent of lilies, and
high in the sky tiny silver sickles
carving up the world.

RUBBISH

Melanie Amri

Litter is human blossom,
urban potpourri.
It falls from our fingers like a benediction,
transforming dull pavements
into canvases of joy.
We drop it with love,
as a token of our affection
for the world.
Gaze now at those plastic bags
floating past vast tower blocks,
like angels borne aloft
for our delectation.
Or see them caught in winter trees –
huge confetti silhouetted against the sky.
Is that not pretty, is that not fine?
Is it not wonderful to watch
coffee cup lids windsurf
across a smooth station floor?
Is there not beauty in a crushed can
as it spins and scrapes?
And how else would we notice
the patterns the wind makes
in city corners, when a gust whips
wrappers against the wall.

Litter is the ultimate democracy – free and available to all.

SWEET IDLENESS
*(after the painting 'Dolce Far Niente'
by John William Godward 1861–1922)*

Frances Sackett

Oh yes, of course, my goddess wears these well.
I brought her many riches, truth to tell,
when visiting the Orient. That marble pool
she languishes beside was shipped to Liverpool
from best Italian mines. She dips her hands,
then lies and dreams on skins from lands
she'll only hear about when great men talk –
boast about adventures when they stalked
out animals for ivory and furs.

That passion! She's almost like a cat that purrs,
and in her idleness she must be glad
to know a man like me. I've had
the spoils of wealth. She's one. The painter's art
can only show what's there: munificence of my heart.

POETS CORNERED

Bruce Newman

My first, flamboyant and eloquent
Blossomed in that Big Apple
Where his meteor blazed and died
Spirited away into that good night
Resolute, dissolute, bleary-eyed, deified

My second loved the Fox and Horses
Because nature's mild and real life's bitter
Like the death of the tragic Plath
(The guilt started, the pen stopped)
And its terrible aftermath

My third, just like his Skylark
Was a bit of a fly-by-night
Waxing lyrical, satirical, political
Until the Spezia sea drowned him
And the Eternal City found him

My fourth lorded it o'er land and sea
All the way to Missolonghi
Nowadays he'd be a tabloid cert
With a lover for every Don Juan verse
And an unsilenced Lamb dishing the dirt

My fifth was busy peering
Out of High Windows (what's your game?)
And turning out four letter guff
But now he's lauded in the Culture City
For serious literary stuff

SHAKKEI – BORROWED SCENERY
(Tatton Park Gardens May 2016)

Joy Winkler

Take the perfume of wallflowers,
a sundial, stone lions, spaniel's tombstone.
Take the shape of topiary. Take the word 'topiary'.

Take white paint on rotting wood;
the smell of turpentine, sting of a blowtorch,
condensation on greenhouse windows;
write your name on them.

Take flanks of silence peppered with bullets
of laughter. Take a cloud and drape it
over children playing.

Take the wings of Magnolia, bowed
heads of ferns. Take the forest.

On second thoughts put the forest back.

Take ducks mapping water lilies,
ripples that distort the rust and gold
of rhododendrons. Take the bold
brush-stokes of Azalea.

Draw in a longing for meadows, yellow
as butter. Draw in earth smell, the stench
of Hawthorn; edge the pond with them.

Take the bark and squeak of moorhens,
an echo of thunder that was once
a fairy tale; let it drag its watchful net
through the stillness of reeds.

LIMITED EDITION

John Paul Davies

The sea loathes the iron men,
seeking to rust his replicas
sunken inshore, marking his years.

The steadfast men a breakwater,
each age a serial-number
branded at the nape.

One howls mutely in its iron cradle.
Horizon blinds Eighty, a death-mask rehearsal.
Two tries to run, its head too heavy.

For his Fortieth edition
he cocked a finger and thumb pistol,
melded the iron gun to his temple.

Now Forty lies in the lolling dunes,
gaping at the bird-strewn sky,
crab emerging from its hollow skull.

Beyond his formative years,
the beach stretches statueless;
untainted sand doubts his existence.

Water rises to the hips,
sea blisters wrought skin;
breath trapped in the iron ribs.

Bones dissipate, rust creeps,
until even the tallest he ever was
disappears beneath the iron sea.

THE DARKROOM

John Paul Davies

Red water laps, a familiar form sharpens;
my out-of-focus hand refills your glass.

Toasting the turn of a year never lived,
no one hears the shutter flex

but you, turning to the camera
in miniscule movement, time-lapse:

a wink broken down to its constituent parts,
smile expanded to its own universe.

Brown eyes speak of your resurgence;
recognition in the grey hair

still combed over sun-starved ears,
last reserves of black patrolling the scalp.

In the resurrection machine of the darkroom,
scenes choose themselves in the stop-baths,

chemicals stir the electric memory
and the final image is pegged up to dry:

the roll-up you meant to smoke later
resting on your armchair,

the glass of whisky a third full
relinquished, falling forever.